World Stage Press
Verse from the Village

between
good
men
&no
man
at all

pam ward

World Stage Press
Verse from the Village

World Stage Press
Verse from the Village

Between Good Men & No Man At All
Copyright © 2021 Pam Ward
ISBN: 978-1-952952-21-0

Cover Painting © 2021 Hana Ward

World Stage Press
First Edition, 2021

Printed in the United States of America

Cover Design by Pam Ward & Krystle May Statler
Layout Design by Krystle May Statler

Dedicated to the ones who escaped
and those still in the trenches.

When you came after me,
I was locked in the car.
You smashed the window with a crowbar
but I drove off anyway.
−Ai

contents

Why My "T" Sticks

He threw a typewriter
at me
from the upstairs
front window.
"Now use that in a poem
you bitch!"
So I did.

Ask Lucille

for BB King

Ask Lucille
about stomach muscles
pressed against wood
and how good a man feels
howling in pain.
Feeling him gyrate
feeling him hold
your wide guitar hips
feasting on belt buckle
armpits and sloppy wet skin
hotter than ten kitchens
cookin' nothing but collards.
Singing about starvin'
or sippin' your last shot of gin
or sleepin' in the cold
hotel room of his car.
Lucille saw
Lucille felt
the ache of BB's bones.
She watched poems
squeeze like wet dreams
from folds of a fatback neck
relished his low mannish moan.
"The thrill is gooooone,"
the thrill has gone away."
Ask Lucille about the road
and those clubs who stole their pay
the jive talk, the Chitlin circuit
the weeks without decent work
the nights she became weapon
a stick in a barroom brawl
her neck squeezed so tight

she stayed out of tune for days.
"Paying the cost to be the Boss."
Lucille saw
Lucille felt everything first hand
the wild nights
the hicks with guns
an orchestra of other women
Mahogany, Maple, Ash
the real ones who bore him sons.
"Hold On I'm Coming!"
The heartache that penned ballads
in raspy refrains
songs only grown people know.
Where music becomes your medicine
your confidant, your friend.
Where the show must go on
whether you wanted to or not
playing daily
playing duets
playing through good times and bad
a slow-dance lasting decades
a love story in 12-bar chords
a romance between a man
and a woman's wood grain soul.
Ask Lucille about BB
and she'll flash a loyal smile
but you'll never get her to talk.

The Wig

Something about being beat
bad as a kid makes you drool
when some cruel shit rips
somebody else's neck.
It was the day I found
that dollar blending
in the grass after school
some fool's lunch money lost.
I scooped it up checking
to see who was watching
when I caught the tail-end
of a pack of kids
racing full force
toward 54th street.
Back then a group meant
a fight had broke out
so I ran down to
check out the action.

Jackie wore a grape wig
in fifth grade
fluorescent like those
Jolly Ranchers sticks
spiked rigid, badly fitting
her head it was way too big
and we laughed saying
it was probably her mama's.
Lisa said she had this skin
disease that caused all
her hair to drop off in
large clumps and we always
thought it was cancer
but that didn't stop us

from following her home
calling her Bee-hive
Bullet-head
or Purple Brain bitch
in that mean sing-song
chant that kids tease in.

Phillip Brown and Imit Ricks
had her cornered in the back
of Holy Name's parking lot
holding books to her breasts
like a modern day Magdalene
praying to them 'please stop,'
tears hammering her dress
everyone screaming,
"Just take it off! TAKE IT!"
Imit pushed her good
and she tripped to her knees
her homework wept from her arms
as he pranced around and danced
smacking her upside the head
ranting & cursing like crazy.
Phillip had the wig in one hand
standing over her like God
and she's clutching it with both fists
her toothpick thin arms
working good not to lose it
and she begged them, "please quit,"
like we did when he whipped us.
But that's when Imit
just ripped it right off
bobby pins shot through the air
her whole face a sad
awful wreck as it went
tossed to a corner like a prayer.

I remember we all got real
quiet after that, gawking
at the horrible bald
patches of droopy strands
hanging limp like a street dog
and I walked home
not wanting to go in
and hid in the yard
holding my dollar
pitching small rocks
at the fence.

the last buzz before death

people around me
are dropping like flies
I don't know why
but it seems like folks
right and left have been dying.
Daddy's gone
two grandmas went
back to back
my friend's mama
dropped dead last June.
Flies are a lot like death
the way they crave the sweet
the way they hover over
what's been cooked.
Take Mr. Smitty up the street
he was this ol' timey
shit talking
Friday-night wino
who lived in this flop
by the alley.
Hoodlums & crack-heads
would crash at his house
front door was a regular swarm.
Stayed torn up
stayed red-faced
from midnight till noon
booze oozing out
of each overripe pore.
Stole a whole case of Jack
during the '92 riots
folks racing in while
the liquor store blazed
phone poles lit up

like great big Christmas trees
place was a regular hive.
I watched his barefooted swag
down our street coming back.
One smashed by his toe
but he grinned and kept steppin
singing "Jingle bell, jingle bell, jingle bell rock"
face looked like he'd hit the Lotto.
Used to stop by my place
to chit chat and kill time
told me, "One day I'm buying you
a great big steak dinner.
Yes, siree," he would wink
between long juicy swigs
and huge gnats making love to his sleeve.
Now I wished that I did
that I wouldn't have waited
or worried so much
what the neighbors would think
seeing me in the seat
of his red jacked-up van.
He used to come real early
and watch me pull weeds.
"If you were my woman
you would never do that."
He was sweet
and real old
but still Romeo fine
with his tomahawk nose
and high cheekbones dug deep
in some black backyard
barbeque skin.
I should have gone
took the chance
made that fool grin his
crazy-ass Wild Turkey smile.

Should have went
grabbed my keys
let the front screen door smack
should have laughed
and drank scotch
over grilled filet mignon
should have gone
let the neighborhood
buzz if they want
let them swarm
let their fleshy tongues
fester like maggots.
Should have looked dead at life
zeroed in on the moment
like a fly does your plate
when you're eating outside
like your arm
like your fist raised
and gripping the swatter.
Should have told the man yes
while the day was still young
tasted steak in my mouth
before night buried dawn
before this dry-throated
thought of him gone.

Jeremy Strohmeyer

Dedicated to Sherrice Iverson, Enis Cosby and all those who never saw him coming

When the Devil checked
into the Primadonna
he had on a baseball cap
some Nike shorts
a nasty ass t-shirt with
both nipples pierced
which he showed
to the whole hotel crew.
Checked in under the name Strohmeyer
and strolled straight to the arcade.
Had a poker face
a handful of nickels
and a filthy mind.
Eyed the black girl
playing alone
like last night's meat.
Fed her coin after coin
lifted her up to the machine.
See, the Devil was so helpful
had that Cherry Coke grin
hiding rotten capped teeth.
Copped a couple of gin and tonics
and was well on his way
to that fake I.D. high.
He felt good.
He felt free
like that first sight of Vegas
in the black desert night
like the dice rolling nothing but sevens.
The girl was so glad
to have someone to play
there was patty-cake

freeze-tag
hide-&-go-seek.
They laughed all the way
into the bathroom.
I ain't lying
cuz the Handicap sign saw
the whole bloody thing
those fingers
those clothes ripped
and thrown to the floor
her scream smothered shut in his lap.
He sat on her
smashed both her feet in that bowl
held her whole body down
in that wet filthy grave.
Oh, the paper towels cried
couldn't take anymore.
The Wash-Your-Hands sign looked away.
But ol' Strohmeyer sat
still as death
didn't move
watching old ladies
walking back in and back out.
Snapped that young black girl's neck
like some folks slap their cards.
Snapped it twice he said,
"Just to make sure."

See, this is an ugly poem
a poem for parents
who gamble on faith
leave their babies outside
left like big plates of food
a dog pan, a bone
any ol' hound can sniff
leave them playing alone

and their only defense
is a room key, a Coke
and a dime.
See, this poem is a prayer.
This poem says beware
be alert cuz the Devil's nearby
always hunting for food
always looking for you
or your wandering tots
got a white ice pick smile
and a stack of trick cards
a fat boyish grin
and a criminal mind
a nail file and huge jagged teeth.

Carjackin' Heaven

I used to date men who lived
at the corner of 43rd and pain
men who'd suck
the nipple of my purse
till it bled
till it snapped
till it cracked like cheap vinyl
sliding 25 miles
down the sidewalk
of no love
and no left
and not a through street
with nothing to breathe
but these high octane
fumes of he's gone.
But that was yesterday's blues
before you passed through
you who drove me
all the way to the intersection
of suck my toes
past the dope man's grin.
A be-bop cat
an acrobat
who sprang
from the kitchen
of "come right in
and help yourself."
Sometimes we meet for
joyrides
or street fights
or midnight strolls
down the concrete of fate.
But lately

it's been Mercury
or meteors
and satellites
taking me higher than Sly did
or Bird does
or Snoop's juice and gin.
And men wonder why
my back seats are so plush
why I always run smooth
why I groove
why I step with this sway.
I say hey!
I'm a road
on a cool summer's eve
and all of my asphalt's been paved.

Exhaust

She detested it.
Right down to the
ride up there.
Counting Denny's
signs and cars
broke down.
The fake Aztec
look of the suburbs.
It reminded her
of thin
see-through
curtains
chipped
rotten tile
that smoky
dead smell
of motel rooms.
And why
she left him
for good
she thought
that time
all the busted
up plates
stacks of
ripped pictures
her good dresses
shoved in
the trash can.
How he called
her again
and again
'til she finally

picked up
his voice
in one smog
oozing plea.
And the only
thing worse
the only thing
worse than
that dry
separation
was being
with him now
on this hot
vinyl seat
on another
long ride to
his mother's.

Drop it like it's hot

If you've ever dropped your daughter
alone at the mall
Fifteen. Ponytail. Lipgloss & jeans.
Dropping her alone "to shop."
Dropping her unleashed to meet "a friend."
Leaving her scrubbed, shiny & young
a pan of hors d'oeuvres, wearing her
died & went straight to heaven grin.
If you ain't never cheesed a lie
waved & said, "Bye, ya'll have fun."
Did the long fake-out waltz
like you strolled to your car
doubling-back, watching them
stop at Hot-Dog-On-A-Stick
where their soft kiss spears your own lung.
Becoming bloodhound, watching them roam
stalking through coats, shoes or scarfs.
Becoming mall-cop, espionage Mama.
A female James Bond
feeling a time-bomb tick in your bra.
If you've ever clocked a walk
hunted behind T-shirts & feet
feeling the raw heat of murder
while smelling fries and Dior
teetering between slaughter
and Lord please, make the boy sweet.
Creeping around Footlocker
or Starbucks corners
pretending to like shit you don't need
eavesdropping while pretending to read.
If you've ever dropped your daughter
and fell on all fours
sniffing up pretzel blood

letting your hem lick the floor
forgetting you wore a skirt
stifling a growl between molars
hounding See's Candy teen love
going store after store
then baby, you ain't never lived.

The Affair

back hunched
at the wheel
he veers over
the pavement
recklessly taking
3 lanes at a time
knuckles bulge white
in pulled tight skin
he slams the brakes in
leaps out
yanking open the
passenger side
dragging her
to the gravel
she tries to
twist free, but
he's got her
wrists rips
the arm off
her sleeve
she back-kicks
his shins spiking
heels at his feet
he throws a fit
slaps the shit out her
branding each cheek
with his wedding hand
sunk down to dirt
she grabs for sand
flings some
to his eyes
flies back
to the ride

swoops up
the 110
clicks the
lighter in
thinkin' damn,
why'd I tell him.

Anais' Husband

I met Anais Nin's husband
dog-eared and stooped
holding old bags of her books
which he donated to
the Woman's Building
where I worked.

I'd already read
most of Nin's stuff.
Sex with Miller
Sex with Father
Sex with Chicks
I couldn't get enough
each diary entry, a peeled grape
gushing with the kind of carnage
my college days had yet to taste.

A self-published vixen
she was the queen
of the mimeo machine
running off copies
running through bodies
living a bi-coastal life
with two husbands
one New York and LA
and enough drama
to keep the "lie box"
tucked in her purse bursting
with carefully penned adlibs.

"Did he know?"
I asked my coworker
watching him shuffle

down Spring Street,
one of L.A.'s filthiest
carrying a big, lifeless sack
strapped to his chest
empty but heavier
much heavier
since her death.

Love Poem to Paul Hill*

All right, so okay
so you want to get funky
got your panties all bunched
and your dick feels big
and your prayer books
are feeling like bricks now.
So you bad
you can walk in
and blast a whole clinic
cuz you even think
God's got your back.
Preaching righteous all night
'bout the value of life
plant some bombs
and kill 15 by lunchtime.
You ain't pro-life
you low-life
but check the score, son
we won, own it,
claimed it in Roe vs. Wade
you're just pissed
cuz we won't give it back.
So go home
pull your tampon out
lick your bone solo
take a Midol, a douche or a nap.
Get your hands off my crotch.
Get your lips from my oven.
Get your anti-choice
murderous ass out my house!

* *Paul Hill killed a physician inside a church.*

Single Mom

Somewhere between
a burnt marriage
a greasy kitchen
and a grey 22.
Sandwiched between
these smiling kids
and my painted teeth.
Somewhere way off
from coffee mugs
stained with yesterday's
paycheck, rent due
that last final kiss.
Choosing between
Disneyland or
Sybil Brand*
murder or Mr.
Toad's ride.
Driving all the way
from Anaheim to LA
anxious as an inmate.
Passing your house
your new car
your girlfriend's red bike
smashing the snails
on my porch.
Somewhere between
what I didn't say
and my black
Ajax mouth
scrounging for words
but spitting a shoe.

* *Sybil Brand was the name of a women's prison in Los Angeles.*

With two of you
in my back seat
sweet dreamy lugs
tasting of grape juice
and cherry.
Somewhere between
their breath at my neck
or them asking for water
or the fear
they'll call some
bimbo mommie
gnaws at me yanks
me straight back
from the brink
makes me face
one more sink
full of dishes.

The Chase

I loved it when he let me drive
flooring it, honking revving at stop signs
daring to find crazies to race with.
It really pissed him off.
He could never just chill and just cruise
had to act like some Driver's Ed teacher.
"Now slow in that turn, you know that's our exit
calm down, you don't have to drive childish."
Rule after rule, like I don't know roads
like I can't see streets
like we'd end in the boondocks or something.
Always back seat driving, nail biting
blabbing 'bout some crap I didn't do right!
And don't get in no fights!
One time these cornfeds cut me off in Orange County
chased our ass all the way to Riverside.
Me yelling, "Fuck you, you ignorant pricks!"
Waving my Toys-R-Us pistol.
Back and forth zagging in and out traffic.
The big one is clutching a mallet.
Boyfriend just freaked when he saw that.
"Now, see what you did, you no driving fool
those assholes are going to kill us."
I downshift to first, watched them fly
past my window. I blew kisses then yelled out
"You dumb fucks!"
We got off the ramp but they followed us up
me screaming, "Come get me! Don't make me get out.
I got something here for your ass!"
Stabbing my black plastic gun in one's face
jabbing the other the finger.
Big one leaped out when we got to the light
pounding wild like some maniac landlord

yanking the latch kicking the fender
calling me all kinds of bitches.
I drove fifteen odd miles before they finally gave up.
Lane changing boyfriend just yapped the whole way
called me everything, every damn name in the book.
We were way the heck out in the boondocks.

The Hollywood Sign

Each day I leave home
I see Hollywood's sign
straight up Sixth
underneath Venice
a quick costume switch
where Rossmore
transforms into the cement
stars on Vine.
Where the lip of ambition
is a gum wrapper now
a black sticky mouth
on the base of a shoe
the only speaking part
some folks ever know.

Hollywood
greets me daily.
It teases my fate.
Makes me think
of Grandpa
playing in *Baretta*
telling me Robert Blake
was the nicest guy
but definitely the type
to off his wife.
And how easily
the scene could change
in our own living room
if Grandma didn't stand up
and put her foot down
when Grandpa tripped
and almost ran off with
Dorothy Dandridge.

The sign
bright & clean
screams the word
"Hollywood"
at my car.
A command.
A noire curse.
A drill sergeant
barking Marines.
Smacking me silly.
Yelling at me "hey,
stand up straight,"
A verbal Check-Point-Charlie.
A literary *Star Trek* fleet.
Holding the whole porn industry
from seeping back into L.A.
with only nine letters
a few nicks from sky.

Hollywood laughs.
Hollywood winks.
Bathes me in white
popcorn lies.
Watches me race
just like O.J.
over action-
packed streets.
Watches me swerve.
Watches me streak.
Watches my savage life go by
gripping my coffee
between my knees
wearing my work clothes
like a disguise
trying not to lose
my life around

blow-up doll curves
drivers who get
Clockwork Orange mean
or Christopher Reeve
making bets for my spine.

"HOLLYWOOD!"
the sign shrieks
casting away
Cape Fears or
Boogie Nights.
It sees...Charlie Sheen
"winning"
Spike Lee doing
the right thing.
"Hollywood like you should!"
Kool & the Gang sings.
A burglar alarm.
A high-pitched whistle.
The kind only heard by dogs.
Calling all bitches
and broke down punks
and even drama queens
like me
wearing my sunglasses like a smirk
eating Doritos Nacho Cheese
where an empty gas tank
is the only comedy I know.

And even if I fall in a pothole
or forget all my lines.
Or I'm beaten within an inch
of my life like Rodney King.
And my Hollywood,
a bottle of nail polish,
spills like blood on my thigh.

A slasher flick.
A *Chainsaw Massacre*
fading to Black Dahlia wine
turning into a two-part
cocktail mix of the word.
Holly: toxic berry
Wood: splintered tree
Making me as queasy
as a Catalina boat ride.

All I do is look up
see your giant
gate-mouth smile.
Munching a Bon Bon
Sipping some Vodka
Handing me another
Red Vine dream
Doing your *Hollywood Shuffle*
between drought ridden trees.
You sneak in the way I used
to in Grauman's Chinese.
Quiet as vial of Botox.
Firm as policeman's jaw.
Talking me down.
Telling me, "take it easy."
Handing me
a *Map to the Stars*.
You stand
like *Godzilla*.
The last scene
in *King Kong*.
Shirley McClain screaming,
"just give her the goddamn shot!"
Your 45-foot landmark.
A single word speech.
An omen.

A playlist.
A ventriloquist on speed
teaching a galaxy of stars
how to shine.

Hollywood props me up
pushes a toothpick
between my teeth.
Hands me a script
another pair of
rhinestone pumps.
Whispers to me
like Dorothy
before she leaves Oz.
Reminding me
of all that L.A. is
from Kunta Kinte
to Bruce Lee.
From Florence &
Normandie homies
to racist cops
speeding back to Simi.
Hollywood shines
strobe-light pink
gives me a second call-back time
and reminds me
"there's no place like home."

The will to live

September 11th was my ex's birthday.
Brotha was a bomb scare too.
He moved me from half sleep
to full terrorist alert
turned our home into a battle-zone
of ripped clothes and smashed plates.
But I made it through, okay!
Got me a bulletproof vest and
a car alarm out of there.
Not trying to be glib to the folks back east
but real peace starts in your living room, ya'll
from your driveway to your back porch.
So don't be driving through LA
with your red, white and blue
beatin' Mexicans lookin' Bin Laden to you
bombing mosques all while singing
"Oh, say can you see,"
thinking you got a hall-pass to hate.
Y'all kill me with your $5.00 patriotism
scattering over these streets.
The KKK waved their confederates too
from the back seat right next to their shotguns.
Same kind I cocked at my ex late that night
when we both learned about war
and the art of living through hate
surrendering to our own ways.
I ain't trying to be anti
but don't be waving your flag
and be beating your wife.
Don't be standing on the streets
talking about being a hero
when your ass is wreaking havoc at home.
This ain't about war anymore anyway.

It's more like standing for something
you can bite in and taste
believing in something
beyond bombshells and graves
sucking hot fuel from a woman
with nothing but heart
and a hell of a strong will to live.

Suckerpunched

It never fails.
Every time you think
you'll just lounge
you'll just stay
and lie down for the count
and just bask in that
sure felt good glow.
No, that's when they
leap up, zip pants
lace their Nikes
click the ball game on
or CNN news
and hand you your bus pass or shoes.
But it never fails, girlfriend
when you pull a Mike Tyson on them
when you do the whore move
roll over and get your car keys
before they come good
walk with the sure-footed strut
of a ring girl
and say "bye" without batting a lash
they act like they've been jabbed
had their face splashed with water.
They act like you kicked out their wind
looking stunned
clutching blankets
all close to their chin
saying, "You're leavin'?
You're just going to jump in your clothes?
You're just going to fuck me and leave?"
And them left hooks start flyin'.
And they hit you with lines like
"But baby, my sugar sweet pumpkin pie love

please don't go." Lip to ear
he starts whispering, "baby...
we'd sure make some pretty fine kids."
You'll switch roles.
He'll switch channels
find a good flick that's on
ask if you've had something to eat.
So jump bad
jab 'em quick
if you want to stay long.
Act as bold as the wild
steely locks of Don King
cuz the one on their feet
calls the shots.

What Miles Thought He Heard Cicely Say

"Gimme a black eye
a boot kick
a side of smacked face
a chocolate shake that
can dislocate spine.
Come on, Miles!
Slap me silly.
Knock me into next week.
Drown me in the sea of
your *Bitches Brew* again
till my skin's *Kinda Blue*
and my elbow hangs funny
and does a dry bump & grind in my sling.
Come on, Miles!
Kick the living daylights outta me!
Wipe the smile off my face.
Wipe the floor up with me.
Make me see stars.
Make me hear Lady Day scream.
Make Coltrane blare from the grave.
Maybe I'll get lucky
and meet my maker this time.
Before your trumpet turns weapon.
Before your horn drums my lungs.
Before my teeth beg my ribs not to breathe.
Come on Miles!
It's *Round Midnight,* we got plenty of time!
Why don't cha beat me within an inch of my life!"

Leashes

Phyllis was hitched to Willy for fifteen long ones.
Time nibbled by like sacks of cheap dog food
little brown rocks Willy crunched on the porch.
Willy was a warped noon-drunk carpenter's flunky
who couldn't nail his trap long enough to keep work.
He had this flea bag, this 3-legged mutt he called Otis
who'd bark or gnaw fleas on his raw hairless rump.
They lived in this Riverside trailer park dump
metal doors, padlocks, ripped to hell screens
inside was a hailstorm of flies, ticks and ants
Willy got off tossing balls to chained up Otis.
He'd fire them like whiskey bottles over Phyllis' scalp
then he'd laugh, beat his knees caps
when the chain yanked the dog back.
Now, Phyllis worked shelving stock at a Walmart
eight boring hours putting useless junk back.
One night she just snap leashed their house to her Plymouth
with Willy sleeping it off in yesterday's pants.
Hauling the house up a ramp of the 91 freeway
Phyllis unhooked the shack into traffic.
She watched it roll, smack a rail and go into a spin
as if the back-end was chasing the hood.
When the tank blew, a blaze choked-off three lanes
all heart attack red and a mean wino green
burning rubber seasoned her hair.
Phyllis sang *Chain of Fools* by Aretha and left
with Otis panting his own happy tune on the glass.

Sunflower Seeds

for Marlene*

I stole a sunflower plant in front
of the police station today
a wild screaming yellow stalk
fighting a bed of angry weeds.

I snatched it in broad daylight
yanked the root with my hand
grabbed it like it was already mine
carrying it boldly
carrying it royally
like a golden precious staff
or stick
or a baton
like the kind slammed against Rodney's spine.
I marched down the street
in a single lady parade
daring somebody to stop me.

I took the sunflower home
and planted it in my yard
near the barely hanging on broccoli
near the sad and stripped-searched beets
near the carrots that came out of nowhere.
I buried it thinking about my son
and how he likes salty black & white seeds
and how his speeding ticket could've turned ugly
when we picked him up that night
if the officer wanted to trip.

* *Marlene Pinnock was a grandmother beaten by a Highway Patrolman on the 405 freeway.*

I buried the plant with some poems
that didn't amount to much
something about water-boarding
and Zimmerman whipping ass again
but my first thought when I saw it
was of the homeless lady, Marlene.
Laid out on the freeway, flat on her back
weather-beaten and wilted
shielding fist after fist
getting stole on, getting pummeled
right & left hooks to the jaw
with him riding her stomach
riding her gut like a horse
hitting her over and over
again in the face!
Like his uniform transformed him
like he was a king
trampling a black woman like dirt
like mud underneath his feet.
I thought, this lady could be
my own mother, my sister or me!
So naturally, when I saw that flower
I rescued it from the police
because sometimes you just have to
march up to power.
Sometimes you just have to
combat the weeds.
Sometimes you just have to
snatch back what's yours
even if it's just a flower
or a rock in the street
growing like a riot
in the palm of your hand.

Coffee at 3am

Oh, Puerto Rican man
I am watching you over
my wet swollen mug
long covert looks
in the oblong mirror
row after row of sad
hollow cakes
and whole trays
of sectioned off melons
here in this forty watt
den of chewed menus
the cafe of eternal pours
        Oooh, Puerto Rican man
I don't know your language
my spanish no good
and it spends like a peso
on West LA streets
but we speak
the soft swirling
rhythm of spoons
the all knowing soft
lisp of napkins
        My sweet Puerto Rican man
you cut me in half with
those hungry black eyes
and your way-too-tight jeans
where your name sleeps inside
of your hot melted wallet
and I watch you
I watch your smooth
overworked arms
and that snug aqua tank
I watch as my knife aches

my fork makes
that last final jab
and my heartbeat
is sinking the butter
        Ai yi yi, Puerto Rican man
you've caught me this time
my eyelids are freezing
the ink on this page
and I only look up
when a hand comes
lingers a moment
pours me some more
and I thank it
I stir as my spoon
tings the edge
and I swallow
the warmth of it slow.

Barrier Method

I found a condom
by my car, okay!
Smack dab by
my rear door
smiling all bold
from the cold
concrete black
a nasty fat
profolat
wet slimy moon
lying limp like a dog's
sloppy tongue.
Ain't this some shit!
Some low life
just got his did
then tossed
the damn thing
into traffic.
I imagined them
parked in this
very same stall
drawls pulled down
handcuffing hers
at the knees
thighs licking glass
like a squeegee.
And him with
his hairy ass
hanging all raw
and that jimmy hat
rubbing back
in and back out
and then

back in again
on and off
like some cheap
prison light bulb.
Pounding wild
screaming loud
and professing
his love
"Whose got damn
pussy is this bitch?"
and now
here it was
sprawled out
exhausted
leaking
all happy
I stepped up
gunned it hard
and took off.

She Should Have Called 911

for Nicole Simpson

The last episode
left her holding it
loaded
sawed off
and cocked
aiming straight
at the tip
of his manhood.
He stood raw
looking right
in those cold
steely eyes, saying
"Wait, baby. Wait, girl.
You know it's all good.
Now put the thing down
and quit trippin."
He stepped up.
She stepped back.
"Don't you fuck
with me Ray,
I'm not playin'
this time."
It was hard
to see out of
her bloated shut eye.
She could move
her front teeth
back and forth
with her tongue.
"Come on, babe.
It's me, Ray,
your love makes me go crazy."

And he took a step up
"but you're sweet.
You need me!
You're my tenderized meat.
Girl, you're all I got
good in my life."
And his lips grazed her neck
until all her skin thawed
and her hands lost that tense grip of hate.
"Now see," slowly he spoke
"This ain't no way to be,"
and she moaned
and he sighed
and it all felt so nice
until he snatched
the thing
aimed close
and shot.

Hollywood Hills

Every time I went over Kim's her dad came
outside while we laid next to the pool.
It was a small, useless tank
with horrible swamp-green water
where bugs hatched their eggs in the scum.
Her dad would *always* come out there
checking the pump
fiddling with the gauges
sticking his wrist in the deep end.
Kim leaned over and told me
they were all in therapy now
ever since he fucked one of her friends.
I watched him duck in the garage
and emerge later, shot glass red
a Jim Beam smirk on his lips.
He wades in and wet covers his thighs, hips and gut
ballooning vulgarly over his shorts.
His grin made me think of a zipper half-down.
A man whistling at kids while hosing his grass.
My hairdresser begging me to "suck it," right there in his chair.
And I know that it's out there
happening in Hollywood or Watts or Marina del Rey.
Every day there's a hand with a fistful of candy.
A wet hungry tongue resting over chapped lips.
A fist waiting to scrawl your name on the stall.
An arm luring you down underwater.

Breast Milk

*for that racist, crazy fool, Dylann Roof**

Dear Dixie, descendant
of slave ships & chains.
The original midnight creep
creating a whole race from rape.
Hey, Slave Monger!
El Capitan of unclean!
Feasting on hatred.
Slaving ya own flesh & bone.
Home-Wrecker, Cracker
Mr. Burrito White Supreme!
Hey, Blood Spiller.
Yo! Petri Dish of Disease.
Breeder of sons you don't want.
Singer of anthems on greed.
Waving your red treasonous flag
like some sick badge of honor.
Segregationist!
Desecrationist!
Spawn of the burnt-cross lawn.
Heir of the German Shepherd.
Papa Lynch Mob Grenade.
Descendant of nursemaids
suckling breast but taught
to detest her face.
Hey, white boy! Yeah, you!
That fool with the gun.
Killing six women and three men
claiming you're saving your race!
Listen, I know you can't
blame your idiot genes
but stop biting the titty that feeds.

* *Dylann Roof shot nine innocent black people while they were praying in church.*

Le Revue Negre

for Josephine Baker

Before Baldwin lifted a suitcase
before Chester Himes escaped
Josephine packed her bags
& skipped off to France
severing ties with America
an umbilical cord
strangling her neck
she boarded a ship
bailed the U.S.
like bailing the back hand of
a bad, brutal marriage.

This Nubian princess.
This queen of the bait & switch
had everyone going bananas
examining how yellow fruit curves
dancing nude, except for
her produce-section skirt
fifteen gyrating
penis-shaped smiling grins
happily tapping that ass.
While everyone studied
her circumference
which defied gravity & physics
dreaming of banana nut bread
banana pudding, banana splits
Josephine hid Nazi secrets
on sheet music or brassieres
or the ticklish part of her panties.

This Doll-face
This Venus

This St. Louis tease
became the biggest star in Europe.
Twerking her galactic hips
living so large, so vast
so spread-eagle wide
Saturn dropped her shirt
and slow dragged with Mars
causing Pluto to yell, "I got next!"
Josephine lived so big
clothes couldn't hold her back.
Boogilooing in her birthday suit
refusing to kowtow or bow
except for her 7th her 10th or 12th curtain call
hoola-hooping till the sun beamed up
or like bloomers fell back South
touring London, Paris, Rome or Berlin
showing the whole world
how black girls got down.
Not with dust mops
not in aprons
not the back of the bus
but infamously untethered
living high on the hog
buying a *Chateau,* so East
of the West's ugly mess
the fire bombs
the German Shepherds
the strange fruit strung on trees
courtesy of Uncle Sam's
"Welcoming Committee."

As the zookeepers of America
gawked or angrily shook their fists
Lady Liberty did a two-step
and shimmied by the sea.
Hoisting her worn-out gown

lifting teal she screamed,
"I see you, over there, Josephine!
Go on, girl! Get it, get it!"
And way across the pond
nibbling bon bons
ordering prawns
sipping endless flutes
of *Veuve* or *Moet* champagne
The Electric Slide Goddess
blew a kiss to her rusty friend.
"*Mon Chéri,* you need to come back with me."

And all the gorillas back in Africa
eating Chiquitas, beating their chest
doing their best Josephine
between branches and leaves
dancing a Cha Cha
trotting a Rumba
tossing peels in the street
gripping "J" shaped fruit
in their palms like a spear
honoring all escapees
praying for those still caged.
Remembering the black girl
the one with gumption
the nude émigrés
who had the mendacity
to leave her country
Lil' Miss *Parlez-vous Francais.*
A black woman who ran from home
shearing her clothes, shoes & hair
severing herself completely
sailing far, far away
a gold star
lighting the way.

Portrait

You can see when it's hanging
all raw from a tree
lynch mobs assembled
in tall stupid caps
smoking black folks
like they're Tiparillos.
And the moon turns its back
while a whole family bleeds
and those sheets share
the cold smirk of hate.
And the scabs of all that
run so deep, are so thick
they become boils
they become bonfires
they become big gruesome scars
passed from family to family
and picked on and picked
until one gets on your Uncle Floyd's neck.
Now, Floyd was a man
who spent half his days passing
bragging to any ol' fool with two teeth
talkin' 'bout hidin'
talkin' 'bout pullin' the wool
over white folk's eyes and the pride
of being white enough to piss in their sinks.
He married pasty Aunt Fay
had a kid right away
all three with their keen features
peachy cream skin
were the picture
of almost white blackness.
They would pass in pull carts
or out-the-way towns

sit right down and eat lunch at the counter.
But that next year, they had *him*
the son no one mentioned
and the whole family
felt like their sun had come down
that winter they had little Willie.
See, Willie's hair napped
and his skin spoiled their image
reminding them what they tried to forget.
It had been so damn easy
to leave it like food on your plate
to put it away like your mirror or your keys
shut tight in the heart of your purse.
They saw Will as their curse
their blackhead, their mole
and the whole family
chose not to see.
He lived in back seats
told to keep his head down
told to sleep in the car
that cold vinyl grave
while they laid on fresh hotel satin.
He lived with their sickening
obsession for whiteness
the bleach creams, the lye mix
the clothespin on nostrils.
He lived life trying hard not to breathe.
And the whole family blew a huge sigh of relief
when he ran off and never came back.
And I see when I stare at them all
in this picture
all three the color of cotton balls
sucking up dirty water.
Floyd's heavy gut
Auntie Fay in her beads
a doughy girl stuffed in a coat.

But if you look real close
there's a slim half-mooned son.
The picture of pain, hidden
behind his dad's stiff wool pants.
And it's sad when the lynch mob
turns into your kinfolks.
And you're just a scab, a blemish, a zit.
Where hate reigns at home
big as a white Viking stove
a self-loathing flame even the Klan couldn't top
hotter than ten cross burnt lawns
twenty bombed-to-bits churches.
Thirty lashes couldn't match the horror
growing like cancer inside your gut
growing like blood does on gauze
or on bleached-to-death sheets.
No, this kind is harder to see.

Paper Plates

the good ol' days then
were late nights in the kitchen
canned beans and weenies
and fries cooked in fat
war food that talked back
and thrashed in hot grease
and popped if you got up too close
but we loved it
loved standing there
right next to mom
near the comforting warmth
of her house dress
we stood watching hotdogs
exploding like welts do
gruesome skin oozing with juice
near the flame
near her elbow
we stood there
in peace
and the quiet
of daddy's not home yet.

Poor Reception

Before life became static.
Before TV sets
that never turned off.
Before Jim Beam nights
with the six o'clock news
you snoozing off
with the sports page
the want ads asleep
in your lap
while your shot glass
stayed wide awake.
Before layoffs
and cutbacks
and 9-to-5 clean-
shaven days
became beards
before your uniform
turned to pajamas.
Where you sat
in dim rooms
with a full concrete view
of the broken glass
still life of alleys.
Where your kids blistered
wearing their way-too-small shoes
the food stamps that came
but just never quite made it
and it all made you
just want
to drink yourself blind.
Before then.
When you worked.
Way before all the storms.

When the whole world
was warm and felt
summertime good
and Friday's paycheck
felt like God.
And your pockets
had dreams
that could Cha Cha at night
and life never blurred
or got fuzzy from static
back then
the reception
was good.

Visitation Night

Not the pit bull on the front lawn.
Not the chain link fence.
Not the bars on the back door
or the new address.
Not the deadbolt she opened up anyway.
See, when Waymond came
when Waymond aimed
his VW toward her door
revving the porch
smacking his horn
mad as all blazing hell
mad as postal workers forced
to work triple shifts.
He looked bad, like a crackhead
but couldn't care less
and the moon watched
like somebody waiting in line.
Waymond lost his damn mind
pitched a bitch and turned into a bona-fide fool.
See, when Waymond came
it was typhoon and hard shoes
thunderbolts boomed under each
hard mannish stroll.
Stepping quick quick quick
drumbeats rolled out of each stride.
Not the parole board.
Not the punk boyfriend under the bed.
Not the bathrobes and slippers
who tipped out to peek.
See, when Waymond came storming
with razor-blade lips
talking loud
cussing her out

talking blizzards and downpours
and gang fighting skies
cussed her three damn days straight
felt like eight days of rain
went home, changed came back
said all the same shit again.
See, when Waymond came
he brought lightening
bolts right in the house
and all hell broke
all high-fives and party-time stopped.
And he stood on two feet
screaming tornadoes in the hall
"Them is my kids! MY KIDS!
Call the law if you want!
Ain't no judge alive
fit to keep me away.
Law can kiss my damn ass
when it comes to my son.
That's my blood.
That's my heart.
"Rico! Daddy loves you!!!"
There was gunmetal clouds
broken Coke bottle rain
but the next thing I knew
the sun came back out
and ol' Waymond was gone.
Not the pit bull
the chain link
or bars said a thing.
"Daddy, bye," was the last drop I heard.

The Yellow Children of Monticello

for my cousins, Sally Hemings and Jefferson's descendants

Before Roosevelt.
Way before J.F.K.
Before Clinton claimed, "I Did Not Have Sex!" on TV.
Before Monica Lewinsky tripped out & forgot to wash her dress.
Thomas Jefferson was banging out tots like a fiend.
Making a banquet out of Sally Hemings' body
he created more kids than he could track.
Jefferson kept his black children under lock & key
all while singing "Oh, say can you see."
All his pickaninnies, tall and skinny
looked exactly like him
and nobody blinked.
Nobody batted a lash
seeing these yellow children of Monticello
springing everywhere like weeds.
They heard Thomas' cry for freedom
turn into bedroom deceits.
They watched their father
a boll weevil, feast on fresh drawls
like a cotton gin separating seeds.
And when they realized he would never, never,
never, never, never, never, NEVER, set them free
they read his *Declaration of Independence*
they waited for a harmony of coughs
they watched this 'Apostle of the *Constitution*'
and willed bronchitis to drum his lungs.
They sang hymns to bring on fever
yearned for heart attacks or strokes
ANYTHING to take his last breath.
But Jefferson lived & lived & lived & lived & lived & lived & lived!
"We hold these truths to be self-evident," he said.
For his yellow kids,

this was just a long-winded speech.
People applauded.
People lauded him a saint.
People ignored his children in chains.
Only when slavery began its Swan Dance
unraveling like a hem, did Jefferson finally relent.
At last, finally on his deathbed,
before he peacefully died in his sleep
Jefferson & Sally Hemings' kids were finally released.
But wait a minute! Stop the presses!
Maybe it didn't happen like that at all!
Maybe Sally was fed up with all the laundry, sex and lies.
Sick of the broken promises, maybe Sally finally snapped
like an overseer whipping a child's back.
Maybe Sally had to go "all Monica" on them all.
She wouldn't be the first to topple a president.
Plantation life takes its toll.
So maybe Sally took out Jefferson herself
having that one final pillow-talk at last.

Someone's In the Kitchen With Dinah*

Someone's in the kitchen with Dinah.
Someone's in the kitchen, I know, oh, oh, oh...

That time,
Slavery thought
the meat was too tough.
Flinging a horseshoe
against her skull
Slavery knocked Dinah down
beat her 150 lashes
beat her every day for a week
beat her tied to a tree
without food or water
beat her piñata-style
like Questlove beating his drums
ripped her dress and beat her naked in front of her sons
beat her 'til the moon couldn't stand up and take it no more
beat her 'til the pitchforks & cattle prods started to moan
beat her 'til she screamed, cursed their souls
& finally blacked out
and they still beat her comatose body ten more times
'til the cat of nine broke
'til the overseer quit to feed his dog
'til her back was a slab of ground beef.

This time,
Slavery woke up
hungry for love.
Dragging her to the kitchen
he slammed Dinah against the wall.

---

* *"Dinah" was a generic name for enslaved black women. One June 23, 1855 Celia murdered her enslaver after years of unwanted abuse. After hitting him in the head, she hid his body parts throughout the property.*

A romantic, Slavery liked sharing what he had
clothes pinning both tits
he rammed a liquor bottle up her ass
and some other stuff he found in the cabinet.
And before she ran off
before they noticed the paring knife was gone
before the bloodhounds
the bonfires, the hot skillet mobs
before they saw his bones hidden in the bottom of the pot
everyone was outdone
by the meat she served that day.
Dinah just smiled and said, "smothered steak."

> *Someone's in the kitchen with Dinah.*
> *Someone's in the kitchen, I know, oh, oh, oh*
> *Someone's in the kitchen with Dinaaaaaah!*
> *Strumming on the old banjo.*

Car Fight 59

I like LA, particularly
the car racing in residential areas.
The last one was with this obnoxious slob
in a white gloss Benz.
Cut me off big time.
Him and his fat cigar
and Barbie bitch
glued to his lap.
Passed me with one hand.
I had to brake so hard
my groceries wrecked
the backseat.
It really pissed me off
but I got back next to em
and blasted the most
ghetto rap tape I had.
Slide all the windows down
started bobbing too
like I gave a fuck
acting oblivious
to his dog-faced mug
and stuck-up date.
I waited in the right lane
foot hovering the gas
like a crook
ready to smashed it down
the second that sucker went green.
Wasn't even where I wanted to go.
But sometimes you gotta show folks
let em know
we all own these streets
even if it means
taking in extra scenery.

Haiku for Latasha Harlins*

Hot, all she wanted
was some juice not some gun-hoe
fool shooting her back.

---

* *Latasha Harlins was killed in Empire liquor near Figueroa by Soon Ja Du. Her death ignited the 1992 riots.*

Rioter's Blues

"A riot is the language of the unheard." –Martin Luther King

Baa baa, black sheep
have you any fools?
Yes sir, yes sir
three cops full.
One with his kneecap pressed against Floyd's neck.
Another one just standing dumb, another on is back.
Baa baa, black sheep
after seeing *that!*
we done brung
some gasoline
some matches
and a bat.

Here is something I can't understand

for Trayvon Martin with respect to Cypress Hill

Here is something I can't understand.
HOW ZIMMERMAN CAN KILL A MAN!

I'm just walking home from the store.
Crazy Ass starts a Civil War.
Hoodie's on cuz the street is chill.
Seventeen, trying to get some Skittles.

But here is something I can't understand.
HOW ZIMMERMAN CAN KILL A MAN!

Crazy Ass thinks black skin is whack.
Calls the cops, they tell him, "Stand back!"
Girlfriend tells me to "Run away!"
Hell no, I say, I ain't afraid.

But here is something I can't understand.
HOW ZIMMERMAN CAN KILL A MAN!

Beg and scream for him to let me be.
"Daddy lives in this community!"
Try to fight when I hear
BLAM! BLAM!

and Zimmerman just killed me, man.

and Zimmerman just killed me, man.

and Zimmerman just killed me, man.

Panther Mothers

Dedicated to the mothers of the Charleston church massacre

Oh Mary, Mack, Mack, Mack
All dressed in black, black, black
With 25 bullets, bullets, bullets
Strapped to her back, back, back.
She went to church, church, church.
Knelt down to pray, pray, pray.
Unzipped her jacket, jacket, jacket.
Tapped her beret, ray, ray.
She channeled Huey, Huey, Huey
and H. Rap Brown, Brown, Brown.
She asked those brothers, brothers, brothers
to help her now, now, now!
She didn't want this, mess, mess.
But just in case, case, case.
Mary was ready, ready, ready
with guns and grace, grace, grace.

Say Her Name

We used to call her Miss Ann.
Some call her Becky.
A bossy little cuss
who tossed shoes at our head
the kind of hatchet-face
who sold us down river.
Today we say KAREN
with a capital K. K. K.
These fraudulent little cunts
pop up once a week
demanding to speak to the manager
flapping antebellum tongues
with their fake tears
fake traumatized Avon lies
igniting hate crimes as wideeeeeeeeeeee
as all 50 states
until no man with a suntan was safe.
Karens call the cops at the drop of a hat
black kids selling lemonade
or jogging down the street
or bird-watching alone in the park.
On a lark, 'cause she crazy
or got Cro-Magnon genes
here she go tattling
wagging that finger
weaponizing her pussy....again
pushing her white privilege stank
all up in our face
getting us lynched, tarred or feathered
or burnt at the stake
all while feigning some fake-ass distress.
Don't believe me?
Here's some Karenish shit for yo ass.

Carolyn Bryant had Emmett Till killed
Susan Smith said "A Black man did it."
The Scottsboro Boys were almost lynched
by some lying ass trick
and did I mention the Central Park kids?
Some Karens have gone on to obliterate towns.
Somebody say Tulsa.
Somebody say Rosewood, please.
See her muddy little feet?
Hear those crocodile tears?
There goes Karen playing the same role again
going for another Academy Award.
And wait, stop complaining
stop saying you hate the name.
If Karen's the real victim
then go ahead, flip the script.
How many black chicks call the cops
and send white women to prison?
Go ahead, Cinderella, I'm waiting.
The Karen moniker marks
a legacy of predatory terror.
So if the shoe fits then wear it.

A dog barks in winter

It's three o'clock now
and the mailman
ain't here yet.
I wait and I listen
for jangling gates
and ol' pissed off dogs'
barks ricocheting
off porches.
It's three o'clock now
and the California palm
looks so burnt
in December.
The hot powder sand
has gone cold
gotten rough.
The wind blows
a Frito Lay bag
toward my door.
It's three o'clock now
and the mailman
ain't here.
The neighbors sort trash.
A pick-up goes by.
Flies rub their hands
in my coffee.
The young finch of spring
has grown up and flown.
The freeze makes me close
all my windows.
Why do they leave you
before it gets cold?
Their song like a record
that someone snatched off

and my radio can't get the station.
Why do they leave
right before it hits winter
like a lover who wakes up
to go find a match
walks off and never comes back?
It's three o'clock now
and my mailman ain't here
and I see no sign
of his white
midget truck
or his blue felt tip pants
feet mashing
name after name after name
past dues and big stacks
of dull ugly bills
millions of bright
useless coupons.
It's three o'clock now
and it's cold here outside
but I wait for him
day after day after day.
I wait for him
just like I wait for a check
or my doorbell to ring
or my phone's final song.
Like a bone I sit
although the sun is half gone
and my box is still hollow
and my dog hasn't been home in years.

Black As A Bullet-proof Vest

for my father, James Moore, architect, Watts Library

I grew up entrenched in
all that was beautiful and black
where Afros stood tall as buildings
and fought back the breeze
living in the sixties
with Frisbees and Hula Hoop dreams
spinning around my daddy
trying to analyze his stride
trying to see what lay inside his big size fourteens
a walking heart attack
a living monument
of hot-blooded love.
I hung on his non-slave tongue
watched his ebb and flow ribs.
See, my father wasn't no kowtow
no-greasy-smiling
knee-dance-doing-tease.
No, my father was more of a crowbar
an architect in a neighborhood where
nobody even knew what that was.
Had a white-boy job
when black men didn't mean spit.
Told us to never be anything less than black
proud black, brown black
snow to crow black.
He knew it wasn't about skin tone
because black burned within
each artery and vein, screamed
never apologize
never hide
never longed for or lusted after
or tried to be less.

Our consciousness never was pressed.
Our pride never got conked.
We was barbershop black
Magnificent Brothers*
on a Saturday black
snip snap where afros emerged
to perfection black.
Watts Festival black
marching band black
booty shaking
daddy saying, "Oh my God," black
hot fudge Sunday black
sneak in movies black
steal a lawn mower daddy made us bring it back black
high tops running in a pack black
hide and go seek black
engine engine number nine
going down Chicago line
if the train should jump the track
all we ever was was black.
Might have been liquor store black.
Could have been
crackhead black
but we had razor strap
"Get away from that!
Didn't I tell you not to touch that," black
in yo ass black
but we loved him back
cuz we had Al Green and
Aretha in our living room black
Watts Prophets black
Miriam Makeba black
poetry pounding like drum beats
reminding me to stay up

* *Magnificent Brothers was the quintessential barber shop located in the heart of Leimert Park.*

stay strong
and when the shit got rough
we was pushing right back
Black Panther black
fully strapped
beret wearing
leather jack black.
We was wilding then black
talking back black
don't bring that bullshit
or we'll burn it up black
Watts Riots black
Rodney King black
each knee cap
each step speaks
Florence and Normandie storms
Jefferson and Western rains
60th and Main where mama moved after Watts
hop-scotched all over our tongues.
Chicken bobs through our necks
I speak black
keep my slang seeped in Mississippi
and 99th street pain
midnight spat
always beautifully black
white folks try to pantomime
can't never get it right
selling Pepsi with our pigmentation
as if Pig Latin could ever be French.
Trying to be spooks so bad
some of them Halloween their skin
but black is within.
No copy cat can ever take
what shines deep inside
what beams like a Slauson and Hoover sun
a 103rd street star

a galaxy of Central Avenue jazz.
You can eat a million chicken and waffles and never taste the sweet black
that's lodged deep in the Brillo pad of your lungs
that dances across your mane
that cha chas against your heart
that soothes like a satin lining
in a world of itchy wool face fools.
They will never know slave ships
the ocean bones of our cousins moan
weeping away in their deep sardine graves
floating from Nickerson Gardens
all the way back to the Ivory Coast
but my daddy made me know
kept a library in our hallway of who I was.
I saw my father sitting in his black chair
every night
the one we could never touch
kinky hair illuminated in the bulb
reading, always reading about us.
Stokely Carmichael, Kawme Toure, W.E.B.
Mommy told me to kiss goodnight
but I'm afraid cuz he's holding *Black Rage*
against his chest, ripping through each page
dogged eared from his fingertips.
I go in like a drowned kid facing the wave
peck his cheek because I know he's love
and begin to read everything Daddy put down
even before the words felt good in my brain
cuz all I knew then was Dick and Jane
and popsicle blood on my shoe.
Trying to learn daddy
like a foreign language
trying to imitate his abstract tongue
trying to understand his rage
that could ignite like a riot on a Saturday cartoon June.
Holding his fist like a knot

not because he didn't love us
but because he tired to keep the horror from his house
the cross burning nights
the billy club moons
the snake-pit smile of those
who wouldn't give daddy his due
because they thought black skin didn't deserve squat
and would have shot him in a midnight minute
if they could have gotten away clean.
But he kept building
kept sculpting
kept masons stirring cement.
He shaped wood, steel and dirt
into roofs, floors and walls
creating artwork where people
birthed babies and breathed.
Making structures
making homes
out of slide rules and sludge.
But his best work by far was his four kids
strong black, bold black
we stand as pillars to who he was
all that Watts is
as tall as those towers
as colorful as its art
as luminous as the Watts library daddy designed
beautiful as a Mingus rift
bold as a Cortez line
blowing wind into the building blocks of our spines
wearing our black like a helmet
or a bullet-proof vest
to protect us
to keep our sweet essence alive
so we can walk in a room
and not feel annihilated by fear or shame
cuz inside you're a fortress

a steel pole and a wall.
An architect's daughter
with a twelve-story heart
raging hot
riding shotgun
ready to wreck shop
at given moment
remembering molotovs
and lynch mobs
and streets blazed in fire.
Because Watts is my father
the birth home of my mom
it's a rhythm, a blazing heat
a rock buried inside your palm
keeping the beat
keeping the blood
keeping our history alive
as beautiful as new asphalt
as black as the eggplant sky
laying foundations
one brick at a time.

Baton Lessons

I took two baton lessons and quit
leaving the metal rod
next to the ice skates and bike
I'd already abandoned for good.
It wasn't until Leslie
moved next door that I used it again.
Leslie liked to talk shit
popping her gum in my face
splattering her slob on my neck.
But one day I snapped
ran home and grabbed my baton
put on my pink tights, glitter top
walked back outside
and whooped her right there on the sidewalk.
I remember gripping it
exactly the way I'd seen Willie Mayes
then twirling like in a parade.
Mom made me apologize that time
dragging me down to their house
lecturing about stones & sticks
but secretly I was proud
she'd gotten me those lessons
you never know which tricks
come in handy.

What the body remembers

what the body remembers
what it knows from bone
what it sees with its teeth
in that rent-free apartment called womb.
What the body remembers
what it stores
isn't measured in drums.
It is stirred
in the stomach
that big mixing pot
between fatback and rib
not through ears
but through gut
our third-eye antennae
hiding underneath all our belts.
The body can feel
the slam of a door
the glass that you dropped
when the hospital called
the ambulance scream
police hammering your home
the slow hum a wheelchair makes.
What remains in the brain
can bring blood pressure up
turn your dad diabetic
lock your mama in stroke
leave you all alone
by yourself late at night
with the phone line cut off
your light bulbs burnt out
on the cold kitchen floor of despair.
What we store
what we horde

between muscle and grit
what we pepper our tears with
what seasons our flesh
should be good
like your lover's thighs
wedged within yours
or your children's soft breathing in bed.
Your body recalls things by smell
things by touch
things like home
mom anointing your scalp
cornbread healing air
whole families huddled by stoves.
It remembers your first kiss
your first lick of young love
running up like a whole gang of puppies.
What the body remembers
what we cannot forget
what we sweat out at night
between sheets
between jobs
between hot killa cops
between good men
and no man at all.
It recalls every kindness
every rainbow bouquet
every time someone
saved you some cake.
Your body remembers
how to cure
how to heal itself up
like a mother cocoa buttering scars
every keloid
every sore forming new skin.
It erodes the most lonely
bleakest of nights

with one call out the blue
from a friend.
The body knows how to horde
how to put pain in storage
how to stuff those bad days
into thick freezer bags
how to chew
how to spit out life's bad ugly meat
how to laugh
how to slap
the wet face of self-pity
how to weep when it needs to
how to mend a torn hem
and wake the next day feeling fresh.
It can heal.
It can swallow life's big ugly pills.
It can walk twenty miles
of bad road in the rain
work a forty-hour week
at some dull, deadbeat job
and show up every day with a grin.
See, the body's a woman
who tucks in her kids
fixes piping hot plates
like a fuckin' magician
and she hums to herself
cuz she healing y'all
hums while she ironin'
or yankin' up weeds
every song a rich ointment
a tonic to make you strong.
It can stand in the mud
and still paint a whole house.
It can live on a diet
of thick blood and gristle.
It can bend, arch its back

tilt its throat up to God
say a prayer to each hip
in those difficult moments
taste the moon with its tongue
when the sun has left town
bite the sweet flesh of life
with one tooth in its head
close both eyes and still see
becoming hummingbird
dreaming in eight different tongues.
See, your lungs can read things
written only in womb.
It can still feel its wings
remember rich, painted skies
recall everything
ALL that is pitch-black and good.
See, the body remembers
every follicle speaks
and it never forgets
how to breathe.

Passover Blues

I don't know about you
but I got run-away slave roots.
Roof jumpin' fools
who'd rather rot
than be tied
who'd rather leap
than be horsewhipped
or forced to work free.
Who ran off, escaping
the torture & rape,
or being strung
like some clothes
on the line.

I don't know 'bout ya'll
but my grandma was slick.
The original midnight creep,
she tipped off one moon.
Jumping two stories
all she took from slavery's jaw
was a fat busted lip
and the almighty gall.
Ducking through fields.
Hiking in hills.
Living on snake juice & grime
and "Damn it, bitch
why won't you die?"
Wandering alone
just like Moses
for 40 long nights
until she hit
California's bent spine.

I don't know about yours
but I have blue overseer eyes
and the bondage still taints
the hue of my skin
but I got grandma
black & rich heating
my neck-bones & thighs.
It's a renegade mix
of strychnine & street
a pan of grits flying
for men who ain't right.
I won't bury myself
like some of those
poor lost black souls.
I will flow, red & rich
like a good Seder wine.
Racing like the Pacific
whipping rock into slush.
Always running.
Always coming.
Each wave thunderous & free
with the strength
of a run-away slave.

Stella on Friday

She was walking fast fast fast
boom shaka booty
doing 50
down the concrete
stepping quick
in a halter
and tangerine skirt
she was hurting them clothes
hemline held on for dear life
brakes slammed
pinstriped old men
began to choke
the bus driver sat
and made everyone late
couldn't take his eyes off
that magnificent
boom snap
boom snap
busting out at the seams
stereos tuned to
that 1000 watt strut.
See, when Stella walked by
when Stella's heels
slapped the street
down the block
down to Nix
down to get her month
to month cashed.
Walking fast fast fast
big size twelve's shoved
in some peekaboo shoes
rayon Braille reading ass.
See, when Stella walked through

men thought of holiday food
ham hocks, huge plates
of glistening yams
rice sleeping under some
rich smothered chops
plenty of piping hot rolls.
See, when Stella strolled by
it was Fourth of July
she had fire-crack thighs
and some cherry bombs too
and that booty
that Rhumba butt
directing traffic.
Feet two strong drill bits
just busting up street
hips waxing over
them cross walkin' lines
she walked fast
she walked strong
had a serious purpose
and her eyes never strayed
from the Check Cashing sign
when Stella stepped up from the curb.

To the Sweet lady sitting next to me on the bus

Take me home.
Let me sleep
in the lap of your wallet.
Let my face rub
snapshots of your kids.
Let's eat sunny-side up
fix a batch of home-fries
lay my feet at
the mouth of your stove.
Let's fold clothes.
Let me hold.
Let me feel your chenille.
Let me play in the nest
of your stockings.
Spray me
Jean Nate lime.
Call me sweetie pie
baby doll
your sugar plum.
Braid my scalp to
the humming of reruns.
Can't I come?
Can't I sleep in
the teeth of your comb
near the warm
hollow lip
of your wig?
Let me live
in your pillbox
your magazine stacks.
Let me stay like a stain
in your overworked skillet
the bleach spot

on your favorite dress.
Take me home
my eyes begged
but my lips
never moved
and I watched as you stood
pulled the strap down and left.

Seven Rules on Brutal Fools

A Public Service Prose

RULE 1. **NEVER DEAL WITH NO BRUTAL FOOL.**

RULE 2. **Beware of the Brutal Fool Signs**: Okay, take a breath. Anyone can slip, but if you were ever fool-enough to drag one of these brutes home, at least note the Brutal-Fool signs: screaming, pushing, shoving, criticizing, forcing sex, destroying property, isolating you from friends, driving wild, punching walls, calling you stupid, fat, slut or quintessential bitch (yes, some of these ignorant-ass fools went to college and their evil list of names can be endless).

RULE 3. **Run From Escalating Foolishness:** Brutal Fools are kings at terrorizing and promoting fear. If he stalks you, holds you hostage, throws terrifying fits, kicks the door in, pins you down, takes your phone, computer or keys, remember, Queen, this foolishness tends to get worse. Wait for this ignorant brute to go to sleep then run like Allyson Felix did during the Olympics. Abuse is like mold. It grows fast and you might snap. Lorena Bobbitt sliced her fool like Cato Salami. Though tempting, this culinary feat is not recommended. Better to Usain Bolt and never look back.

RULE 4. **Survival is Key**. If you're dealing with a Brutal Fool, have an escape plan ready. Keep a bag backed. Make extra sets of keys. Teach the kids how to dial 911. Keep critical phone numbers and hard cash on hand. You may need to hop on a bus. If you can't escape, hide in the low-risk areas of the house: rooms with windows, extra doors but avoid risky areas like kitchens. Brutes and steak knives don't mix.

RULE 5. **It Takes A Village.** (Sometimes known as "Call-a-Crip") If you don't have a brother, cousin, uncle or kin, call Ray Ray, Lil' Deadface, T-Bone or Bodine, any O.G. ready to rise-up and check his fool-ass. Brutes are usually spineless mutts who feast on easier prey but flee at the first hint of mannish. This tool has stopped many-a-fool-ass in their tracks. And girl please, don't limit yourself to just men. Call Kisha, Sister Vicious, Tire-Iron-Lynne, Wanda from Compton, Kimmy & Them and "Yeah, my Glock is loaded," Auntie Phyllis.

Rule 6. **Don't Believe the Hype**. After assaulting you, some fools claim their undying love. Others cry Euphrates rivers or strum violins. Some fall to their knees pleading they'll die if you leave or swear they'll never hurt you again. Listen Princess, he's just pimping you, okay. I don't care if his mama dumped him. I don't care if his dad's a dick. I don't care if he swears to Allah or Almighty God or his sobs fill a Las Vegas pool. Even if he threatens to sever his veins or jump off a cliff, or gets a ring claiming "you're the one and only one," trust me, you still won't be safe. These are Hollywood stunts practiced by brutes nationwide. Any woman fool-enough to fall for that okey-doke better go ask Nicole Simpson.

Rule 7. **NEVER Suffer Alone!** Any brute who man-handles a woman is scum! Repeat this. Tell your mama. Tell your sisters, daughters or friends. Blab to everyone, yell at the top of your lungs, "HELP, there's a wild, Brutal fool on the loose!" Put his violent, trifling-fool ass on blast. Don't stay mute. Never suffer alone. Maybe we can save one. Maybe we wouldn't have lost Liz. Maybe the undertaker won't have to work so hard trying to remold your smile. If you ever forget these rules, memorize Rule #1. Maybe like blood leaking through a hospital gown, this time it'll finally sink in.

John Holmes* & Me Just Doing My Job

Mom didn't know what I did for a living
though she dug and found my
good stash of dirt on the floor.
"The Happy Hooker," a dog eared
version of "Behind the Green Door,"
hordes of porn I hid under my bed.
Mom thought I worked at the bank.
I left every day dressed in a blazer
and bun slicked back on my head.
I'd race down the road
let my wild hair flow
switch from corporate to spandex
shoot a right up Crescent Heights
zip through mountainous tits
where L.A. parts its cleavage
and turns into a cross-dressing
dry humping, hot urban sprawl
that everyone all calls "The Valley."
The pork chop.
The backdrop of hot, scumbag flicks
The biggest, the largest
porn capital on earth
and my first real job as an artist.
I pulled in the lot steaming,
sipping wet drippy coffee
licking sweet donut off pinky lips.
The naked face I left home
was now a full blown Cezanne
thanks to Revlon and Maybelline.
I was ready.
John was waiting for me

* *John Holmes, aka "Johnny Wadd" was an actor and suspect in the LA's Wonderland murders.*

sprawled all over my desk.
Not just one John
but dozens of big eight-by-tens:
John with thighs cocked
John with legs spread like pliers
showing his longer than school ruler dong.
And my job,
which I loved,
was gluing John down
pasting him
pressing him into brochures.
There was copy, but come on!
No one cared about that.
All eyes were on his 'Ripley's
Believe It or Not,' penis.
I wouldn't have believed it
unless I'd seen it myself
the enormity
the length
it spit right into physics
almost ruining me for all other men.
In another time, he'd be stuck in a tent selling tickets
some bearded chick strapped to his back.
But John's time was now.
It was the tip of the eighties.
The porn world exploded.
It was growing like crazy
throbbing to unimaginable lengths.
I worked hard
and even picked up a few tricks
but could not help but grin
watching my hands press his shaft
tracing along his wondrous crotch
adjusting, angling it down
to its ultimate advantage.
It was a dream job.

I was a design major
sitting at a drafting table at last!
It felt like my ship had come in.
My art teacher warned
us to never do porn,
"If you do, it means you hit bottom."
I smiled, never revealing
me and John's tiny secret.
I kept quiet and kept cashing
those ridiculously large checks
obscene amounts for a chick
just inches in college
and nobody, not my mom
or my three lucky boyfriends
ever knew what I did
to make ends meet.

Am I pregnant…

"Am I pregnant?"
she thought, walking
her unconscious feet
in the fried, hungry
yoke of the sun.
Wearing nothing
not one thing
but this greasy thought.
"Am I pregnant?
Is this it?
Is this sick
feeling something?
Is that lightness
the slight hint
this heat
or the flu
or some under
cooked meat
not the onslaught
of weeks feeling
nauseous?
Am I pregnant?
cause I didn't
and I could have
used more
something more
something bigger
or better than prayer
and the roulette
half-bakeness
of pullout.
Is that gnawing
that chicken-clawed

ping in my gut
just my fertile brain
teething the question?
Am I pregnant?
am I thickening up
as I speak?
Am I weak?
Is this sweat?
Will I let?
Will it grow
to a diaper
a bib or a wet
Kleenex trip
to the clinic?"
So she asked
with her palm
at the flesh
of her seed...

"Could this be?

Is this it?

Am I pregnant?"

Death Comes

I know about Death
how he sometimes sits
in the front seat with you.
How he watched
when you got in and
switched your ignition
grinned when you fastened the belt.
Death lives in the bone
and the backyard of hope
he cracks jokes when
your blood-work comes
back from the clinic.
He stands near the nurse
who averts both her eyes
while she nervously
shows you your chart.
Death is there.
Death is watching.
His single eye gleams
through the clear test-tube vial.
He smiles while you reach
for your rosary beads
picks his teeth while
the priest blesses the coffin.
Death shows at your door
like an unwelcome guest
strides right on in with big dirty feet
grins while you kneel
while your knees lick the floor
pours some scotch
while your palms sweat
from gripping the cross.
Yes, Death comes

always comes
in the heat of the moment.
He waits like a gurney,
his eyes on the body.
He's that lingering cough
or that festering sore.
He's your own foot
your toes slipping off the brakes
the bone-chilled yell of horns
screeching through blood clotted streets
only to reach you too late.

Below Minimum Wage

She still had the same
half-ass job
at the sweat shop.
Living this sad life
half-way between
savage youth
and the old folks home.
Sewing Guess jeans
below minimum wage
for this dim-wit
sitting by the time clock
who spent whole days
in beauty shops
getting toenails sawed
picking lent off his sleeve
living life wondering
what to wear Monday.
While she sits from sun up
to six o'clock quitting
between baby-sitting gigs
and floors that swabbing
a hit and run car
with half the paint gone
and the heart
to make it
all the way home.

Guilt

Is sitting all day on a long boring drive
to go visit your mother's Aunt Bea
with her old safety-pinned robe
and pendulum tits looking like life
beat the holy shit out of them.
Carving you blue and red bad boozy cake
and the cat fumes make you want to vomit.
Finally it ends, all the maddening chat
and her nasty snot rags, the drooling
the choking, her horrible wheeze
and the breath of pure death to go with it.
Finally, Mom stands, says that we have to leave.
Aunt Bea works her feet, twin skeletal twigs
a fence ready to snap and collapse
"You know," she says slow. "It's so good to see family.
It's been lonely here ever since Ben passed."
And she looks so damn awful, so awfully sad
hair wrecked, missing horror-flick teeth
gripping the rot, sunken porch of despair.
And she stares right at me with her wild, milky eyes
a face of too many nights drunk
a brain struggling to think
and she smiles pecks my cheek
says "you're such a sweet daughter."
And I smile too but look quickly away
like I'm caught at the light
and I see someone homeless
like life's ugly face was there before me
and all I could do was stare straight ahead
and pray that the signal turns green.

Cats and Dogs

It's not how he touched her
sucking her raw
with the sloppy wet gusto of puppies
teeth wildly listing
each thing in her lobe
that his body had already thought of.
Nailing her wrists down as if
she were Jesus. "My God"
how his thighs went to work.
But it's not how he touched
it was more what she thought of
train wrecks and cat fights, gunshots and riots
men drilling holes while you're stuck at the light
the skid marks you see on the center divide
how margarine slides on hot knives.

The Loser

The first time
I thought
I was going
to do it
was at the
Cockatoo Inn
this cheap
hour rate dive
on a red-
spandex street.
It was cold.
I was nervous
chewed gum
while he paid
hid my face
in the moon
of his afro.
I was fully
made-up and got
totally naked
but just couldn't
go all the way.
I don't know why
and he didn't
press it.
I really wasn't
a tease.
But the blankets
were orange
and our skin
just as loud
and the radio
sounded like traffic.

So we rolled around
both of our heads
a sad mess
pressing mouths
until I told him
"Let's go now."
I'll always remember
I left my hairbrush there.
It was nothing big
just a two-dollar
pink handled
brush laying raw
bristles scraping
the table.
I remember wanting
to go there
back to that very room
even years later
thinking I'd get it.
Because even if
it wasn't the brush
or really my first time
something stayed
behind in that room
that I lost
and I never got back.

Inquire Within

You are the big boss
I like to imitate.
You walk across the room
in smooth strides
and hard shoes.
You keep a tight ship, but
I am working late.
I am on the night shift
scribbling notes
licking envelopes
looking for clues.
I am the last boot
on the assembly line
of fat paychecks Fridays.
I am always on time
no intention of
punching out yet.
Will always be
your third foot
your best tie
your large time-clock God
where each click
means more cash.
There is no need to re-negotiate .
I carry my Styrofoam cup
like a porcelain mug.
I take pride in my work
anticipate each task.
I am no ass-kiss
no fast talking
back-rubbing tease
trying to sleaze my way
up to the top.

I don't have to hold
my check for two weeks
wash your car on my break
shop for your wife
bend over your desk
watching ship after ship come in
sending our gigs overseas.
I'm a paperclip
gripped to the invoice of life
trying to survive
trying to float
between drought and high sea.
I'm a good job, America.
Remember me?

Trim

I dyed my hair black, chopped ten inches off
buzzed it straight from my brows to my nape.
Beauty shop chicks couldn't believe it.
"You're cutting all that off?" they asked
as it zig zagged in clumps from my
hairdresser's hand to the sweeper.
"Yeah, I don't want that long hair trip now."
The truth was I was wounded from
this fling the ol' man was having
with this Goldie Locks broad.
I wanted to chop her hair off too.
Had these wild dreams about it
grabbing it, wrapping it around my whole fist
hacking her all the way bald.
Not with scissors either but machete style
with my Ginsu turkey knife, the kind
that can dice bricks of frozen spinach.
The dream was vivid mixed with
wide-mouth screaming by her
spine-splitting agonizing murderous pleas
begging me, hands clenched and gripping her straw
tears streaming over her wet Ken Doll face
the kind my kids cut or poked metal pins in.
And me seething, standing there anxious to saw
breath, beating fast as propellers.
I always woke before I did her.
The beautician brought me back when her blade
slipped and she nicked my throat.
It healed up quick, though, like wounds mostly do.
Not like these memories tinting my brain.
Some stains never come out.

Maid in L.A.

for Hattie McDaniel

Don't let the apron wearing
turban headed, "yassa-massa," fool ya!
Because in real life
she was a butcher knife
a pan of hot grease.
See, Hattie was only acting
pretending to shuck & jive.
While everyone was eating her chitterlings
laughing at her rolling-pin eyes
she had the audacity to sue the city
and actually won
ending covenants restricting
where black folks could live.
Catching hell for domestic roles
Hattie grinned at her critics,
"I'd rather play a maid than be one," she said.
This sharecropper's daughter
This queen of the tongue & cheek
This "maid" was serving up way
more than collards and grits.
When the law banned Blacks and Hispanics
Hattie hollered, "Bullshit!" bought a mansion
and a Remmington 20 automatic.
First black person to ever win an Oscar.
First black woman to sing on air.
See, Hattie was one rare, gutsy chick.

Sneaking Home

One time
I had to get out
I mean out
gotdamnit.
No more sneaking
in the door
easing through
the creek
tipping past
your back
all hugged up
on the blue glow
of the TV.
Or worse.
You cursing
my face
on the front
porch before
I even hit
the door where
all the peeking-
from-the-curtain
neighbors could see.
Cheap wine
in your teeth
bleeding my name
insanity soaked
in your eyes.
No honey,
not this time.
This time I had
my plans made
made a friend lie

saying I was
at her place
away from
your boozy
mouth hollering
cheap slut,
skank 'ho!
No, this time my
purse was packed
with cute panties
toothpaste
skimpy nightie
to wake in, and
when the sun
hit my face
I set hair
in fat rollers
tied a bandanna
tied my Chucks
& some sweats
got dropped
around the block
like I woke
and went running.
And as I jogged up
you were there
hosing grass
so I grinned
trying to sound
winded when
I yelled out,
"Hey, Daddy!"

I'll be Home for Christmas

for Eric Garner and everybody before

I'll be home for Christmas
you can count on me
please have snow and mistletoe
and presents on the tree

While everyone's thinking about ISIS
I'm thinking about us.
I'm thinking of Nat Turner
beheaded for leading the largest
slave revolt in history
dissected and quartered
and stuck on a stick
his spiked head
a vicious reminder
to any slave thinking
about tripping
I CAN'T BREATHE!

See, we got a cancer in America
festering from our country's birth until now
and as chains
turn to lynch mobs
Billy clubs to guns
Black men are getting slaughtered
faster than Zacky Farms chickens.
Black men are killed so much
the U.N.'s investigating us!
Black men been killed so long
they're on the endangered species list.
Come on, I said I CAN'T BREATHE!

See, we got a sickness in America

infecting us from coast to coast.
Florida: Trayvon Martin
California: Oscar Grant
Missouri: Michael Brown shot with both hands up.
Michael Dunn shot a black kid for playing music too loud.
Tamir Rice got shot for playing with a toy gun.
I could go on and on and on and on…
But I told you, folks, I CAN'T BREATHE

America got more love for dogs
than for black folks, ya'll.
Somebody call PETA.
Get that bitch on the phone.
Ask why she's crying about Fido
and not one lost black soul.
Even pit-bulls got more power than us.
Somebody ask Michael Vick.
Somebody call them Katrina folks.
Everybody and they mama saw what they did.
They airlifted all the dogs out there first.
If blacks wanted to leave, they were greeted with guns.
Left 'em with no food or water for 5 fuckin' days
simmering in heat, simmering in sludge
until the Super Dome stank like shit.
I CAN'T BREATHE
I CAN'T BREAAAAATHE

Ask me what color Christmas is in America.
I say red for all the black blood in the soil.
I say white for the only skin that ever seems to matter.
I say green for all the money squeezed from slavery's jaw
and every Walmart employee punching in today.
They burned a cross on my grandmother's lawn in L.A.
Smoked the entire house, neighbors yelling GET OUT!
My kinfolks laid low, held their BREATHE for months.
Didn't I say I CAN'T BREATHE!!!

See, we got a problem in this country
and the story's as old as Moses.
"Reckless eyeballing" got you lynched.
"Be off the street by sundown, nigger!"
And if you ever had the nerve to question
what was done, you got boot kicked
or the street justice served Eric Garner.
Because even when the evidence is right before our eyes
even with the camera lens rolling
or millions of folks tuning in
we still get the same old fucked-up result.
Somebody ask Rodney King.
Somebody ask Trayvon's mama.
Even when we see with our own very eyes
live and in living color
a renegade cop
leaping hyena style on Garner's back
choking a black man to the ground
choking him literally down to death
choking him so hard and so long
Jesus had flashbacks at being on the cross.
Noah had nightmares of being held underwater.
Mary Magdalene wept in her own hair.
Even the Mayor had to go home
and school his son on the ways of cops.
Everyone knows the drill.
Everybody's seen the routine.
Don't make any sudden moves.
Don't say nothing back
and for God's sakes don't ever reach!
This mantra is passed
from Staten Island to Watts.
A survival poem preached
from New Year's Day to New Year's Eve.
A prayer passed from mothers' lips to sons' ears.
A plea so maybe THIS child will live

to reach their next birthday.
A hope that maybe THIS child won't end
up another Abner Loumia, sodomized by cops
beaten to death with sticks
killed for getting their cellphones, their wallets, or keys...
I CAN'T BREATHE!
I CAN'T BREATHE!!
I CAN'T BREATHE!!!

Ask Santa how many white kids get shot in the back.
Ask Santa how many white folks are choked in the street.
Ask Santa how come some folks like Zsa Zsa Gabor
can slap a cop and barely get slapped on the wrist
and while sitting on his lap whisper Santa this prayer:
Thank God for all the witnesses who finally came forward.
Thank God for all the minutes on Ramsey Orta's phone.
Thank God for the coroner getting it right
even if the Grand Jury got it all wrong.

You see, it's Christmas in America
but there's no Christmas for Eric Garner.
There's no Christmas for Oscar Grant
or Michael Brown's mother
and while everyone's singing carols
or hanging ornaments up
the memory of black men
still swing from trees.

Christmas eve will find me
where the love light gleams.
I'll be home for Christmas
if only in my dreams.

You So Muthafuckin Fine

Cut me, muthafucka.
I done given blood before.
There's a petri dish
with tissue labeled "me"
behind some door.

Hurt me, muthafucka.
I done took a bruise or two
living somewhere east of heaven
and the flinging of a shoe.

Love me, muthafucka.
Why is that so hard to find?
Hershey Kiss me
double dip me
suck the slavery
from my spine.
When it's black love
heart attack love
you so muthafuckin' fine.

Remembering Peter

The second time they met
at eleven cause the sitter
had to leave by two
so she really had to
watch her time
and when her husband finally
left for work that morning
fussing out the door
giving orders
like some bothersome fly
buzzing by her ear
she slipped on the little
watch he got her with that
horrible band that would
snatch her wrist hairs and
pluck them right out
jolting her skull
like a bug bite.

This time she remembered
to check her pantyhose
instead of leaving them
inside out like last time
thinking how sweetly he
teased her when he noticed
and those black pumps sunk
all the way down to the wood.
They'd met at the market
on 6th street the day
she ran out of cereal
and had to go out early
to get it. She hated that
market which was really

just a liquor store selling
a few things like corn
flakes and ant spray.
Lots of men hung near
its doors making sucking noises
whenever she walked by.

She had placed her milk
by his newspaper
and the wet jug made huge
spots on the front page but
he just grinned and paid
scribbling his number in
the corner saying, "Call me."
So when her husband
came home and called her
a forgetful bitch because she
left his slacks at the cleaners
she did. And one day
she noticed a large beetle
had gotten in her kitchen
so she smashed it with
the Food Section watching
its fluorescent skin twitch
lifting its legs in a frantic
passion, scratching itself raw
until thoroughly exhausted
quivering to the end
and somehow it reminded her
of Peter, and she smiled.

Los Angeles

Because I inhale LA like the smoke from a Skid Row bum. Because I
grew up near 54th, a million miles from O-Jay's glove, a stone's throw
from Ray Charles' beautiful View Park door, a vision he couldn't see..
Because Mom did laundry singing "Rainy Night in Georgia" off-key,
turning our porch into a bleach and Ajax concert. Because Daddy
drove a Porsche. Because my cousin sold weed. Because my Aunt is a
poker playing fiend. Because the drive to Sin City is best done at night.
Because nothing beats eavesdropping at Denny's. Because I write on
In & Out napkins or gas station towels or the wide, trusty desk of my
thighs. Because Arlington has the biggest dips, and the La Brea Tar pits
are stinky sweet, and coyotes have white diamond eyes. Because Imperial
Hwy escorted me to Cabrillo Beach. Because swimming at the beach
is free and every neon needs black, pitch-black sky. Because EsoWon
Books make you feel like a queen and 99 cent stores make you feel rich.
Because of the fashion show put on by scene-stealing whores. Because the
biggest earthquakes take place on your own kitchen floor if you tangle
with the wrong kind of man. Because cops hit like piñatas, but out here
we swing back. Somebody say, '65. Somebody say '92 riots. Somebody
please pray for peace. Because nothing beats eating churros in the sun
while watching the ballers at Venice Beach. Because Simon Rodia wasn't
satisfied until he touched the sky. Because of Watts. Because of Watts.
Because of Watts. Because of Fat Burger, Tommy's at Rosecrans and the
old-school Tai Ping and the Nisei festival behind Holiday Bowl. Because
a Deuce-And-A-Quarter can make you feel like a star if you're rolling
down Crenshaw at night. Because LA's a "come as you are" kind of
party, and if you tunnel along her veins you'll find everything you need.
As warm as a Tito's Taco, as meaty as a Woody's link, as glorious as a
Slauson sun, as mean as a Rodney King beating, and if you swerve or get
lost or cross over the line, you'll never be too far away.

Barbecue

Allegory for the Los Angeles 1992 riots

sippin on some
looted Jack that
Tony brought back
got me high
and I needed
a taste
to squeeze
in my veins
and swallow the
anxiety in me

diggin down
deep in my gut
like tryin
to bust a nut
you just
can't get
trapped way
in the back
of your neck
hungry
and horrible

teasin me like
that videotape
just a greasy
bone thrown
too far from
the mouth
thinkin we
had it made
till the verdict
it made me sick

cussin at the
television
every click
showin the same
sky-view shit
it seemed
nobody was
filming from
the sidewalk
where I stood
chanting...

the roof
the roof
the roof is on fire
we don't need no water
let the muthafucka burn

mixin my
breath with
the nasty ashes
of swap meets
and midget malls
I got the sudden
and urgent
taste for some
Mr. Jim's
Barbecue

Kitchen Prayer for Grown Girls

Lord knows, I have been a waitress in the
cafeteria of fear for so long.
Scared I'd bed some fool man and ruin my
life. Afraid I'd wake from them lukewarm dreams
of just getting by. Scared I'd face myself
and run! But honey, I'm sick of walking
'round here like I might trip and spill something.
I done hung my closed sign for the last time.
I ain't serving nothing but king-sized plates
of honey here I come. I quit sorrow's
kitchen, I pipin' hot now, and if fear
tries to creep, got my rolling pin ready
my radio on and a recipe
only faith, me and sweet Jesus can make.

Bridge Over Troubled Water

for Guy

Did I forget to say yesterday
when the cash was all blown
or the check didn't come through
or my ballpoint wept its last blue?
Did I forget to tell you
while shuffling through a kaleidoscope of slick
hoping for a *Get Out Of Jail Free* card
instead of a stack of Past Dues
looking for anything, any raft
to keep the nightmare at bay
to keep the change-the-locks
war from my door?
Did I forget, while I was hustling
to keep the wolves off my porch
to keep the hit man from finding
my reliable spine again
to keep from drowning
to keep my head above the abyss
wondering if, wondering where, how or when
I would ever get from point A to B?
Did I forget to tell you
while searching my unfaithful purse?
Cursing the bill collector
or bra-beating my silly ex, again
that yes, I've known Aprils
and apricot moons
and I've bathed in your natural
spring waters at dusk
and I've worn dresses as gold
as a pawnbroker's throat
and I've danced until morning
with only the radio on

enjoyed the sweet tang of hot
codfish you cooked at your stove
arriving like a crockpot of heaven
during a storm.
Because even if I forgot to tell you
you know, dear. You know.
You and I have both always known.

acknowledgments

"Why My "T" Sticks," *This; A Serial Review,* Ohio

"Jeremy Strohmeyer," *The Los Angeles Review*, Red Hen Press

"Car jackin' Heaven," *Calyx: A Journal of Art & Literature by Women*

"The Wig," *Caffeine magazine*

"The Affair," *Hot Water Press*

"Car Fight 59," *The Butcher's Block,* Butcher Shop Press

"Love Poem to Paul Hill, *Sic Magazine*

"Exhaust," *Grand Passion: Poetry of Los Angeles & Beyond*

"Single Mom," *Jones Juke Joint Magazine*

"The Hollywood Sign," *Radius: poems from the Center to the Edge*

"Coffee at 3am," *The Drumming Between Us: Black Love issue*

"Barrier Method," *Scream When You Burn Anthology*

"She Should Have Called 911," *Catch The Fire: Cross Generational Anthology of Contemporary African American Poetry*

"Passover Blues," *A Poet's Sedar: Passover Through the Eyes of Poets*

"Paperplates" *Voices of Leimert Park* and *Calliope*

"Portrait: *Flash Bopp*: Black & Brown Cuidad

"Poor Reception," *Walt Whitman's Beard*, USC

"What the Body Remembers," *Black Women for Wellness, Respect*

"Black as a Bulletproof Vest," *Say It Loud, Poems on James Brown*

"Ask Lucille," *Chiron Review*

"Sun Flower Seeds," *The Los Angeles Times*

"The Yellow Children of Monticello," *Voices of Leimert Park, 2*

"Anais' Husband," Pushcart Nominee–Four Chambered Heart: Anais Nin Poems

"Los Angeles," *LA Weekly*

"Someone's in the Kitchen With Dinah," *Calyx* and *I Didn't Survive Slavery for This!*

"Breast Milk," *Bozalta:* Arts Activism, Scholar

"Panther Mothers" *Poets & Allies for Resistance*

"Le Revue Negre," *Library Girl's virtual tribute to Josephine Baker*

"Kitchen Prayer for Grown Girls," Sonnets At Work

"*Barbeque*" High Performance Magazine–Verdict & The Violence

"Leashes," Main Street Rag

"Remembering Peter," Word Outta Buffalo–Trouble Is My Business

author bio

Pam Ward is a writer, designer and LA native. Her first novel, *WANT SOME GET SOME*, Kensington, chronicles Los Angeles after the '92 riots. Her second novel, *BAD GIRLS BURN SLOW*, Kensington, follows a female serial killer. A UCLA graduate, a recipient of a California Arts Council Fellow for writing, a Pushcart Nominee for poetry, and a Diva Award for community service, Ward created the first anthology of Los Angeles black women poets titled, "The Supergirl's Handbook." She operates a design studio, runs the community imprint Short Dress Press and is part of the fiery poetry troupe, The Ovary Office. Merging writing and graphics, Pam produced "My Life, LA" documenting Black Angelinos in poster/stories. Her multimedia-literary showcase, "I Didn't Survive Slavery For This," a poetic riff on life post-emancipation, was featured at The Leimert Park Book Fair. Pam has published in *Calyx, The Santa Monica Review, Black Renaissance, Voices from Leimert Park, Chiron* and *The LA Times*.

She is currently working on a Watts Writer's Workshop documentary and her third novel, *BURY MY DRESS ON CENTRAL AVE*, the true account of her aunt's dalliance with the prime Black Dahlia Murder suspect, a crime that occurred in Pam's own neighborhood.

www.pamwardwriter.com

Made in the USA
Las Vegas, NV
14 April 2025

20943072R00083